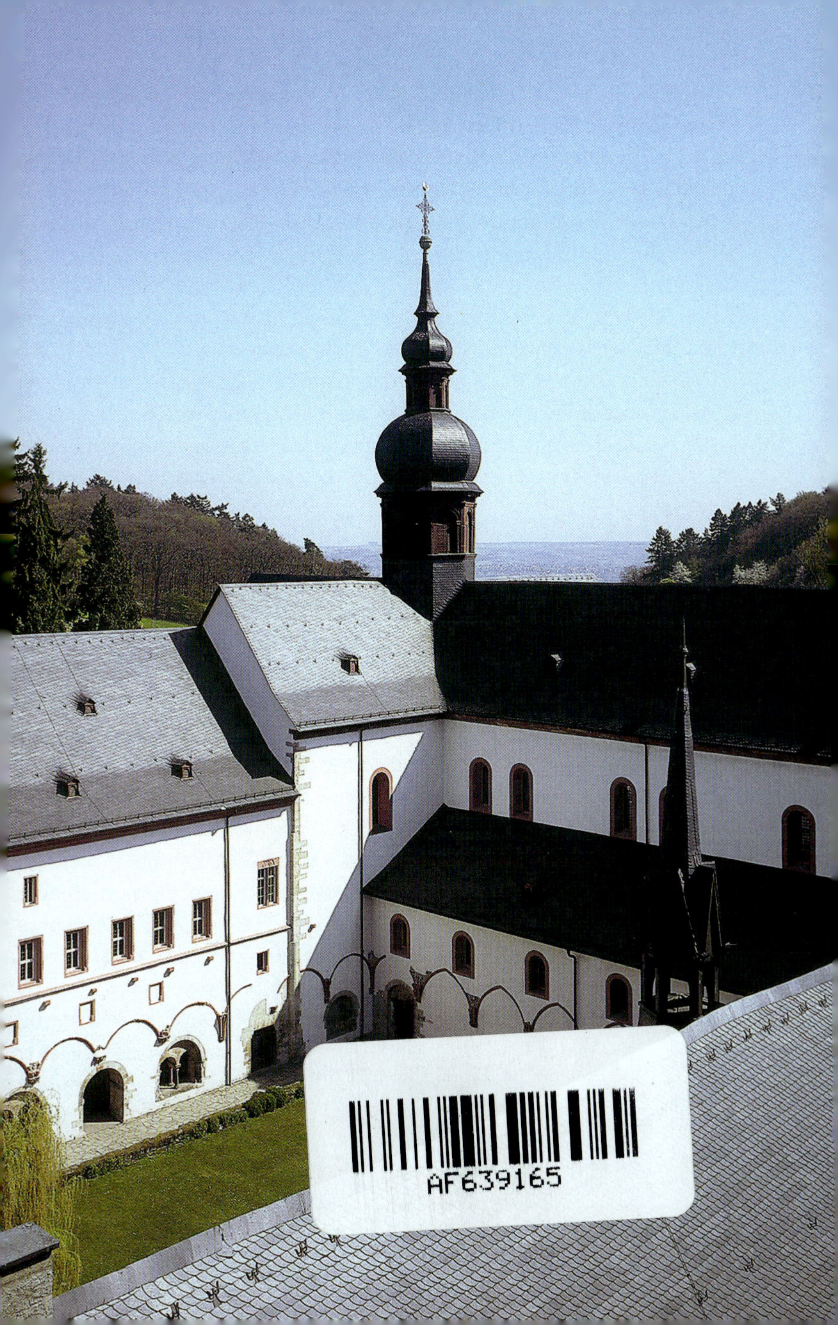

Although the unbending asceticism of the early period allowed no even the slightest comfort, this existence of self-denial attracted many In the 12th and 13th centuries there were at least one hundred and fifty monks and up to four hundred and fifty lay brothers (converses who gained a reputation for efficiency and piety. Their knowledge o agriculture benefited the local population, for the first monks from th wine-growing district of Burgundy further developed the indigenou wine industry, which then formed the most important economic basi of the life of the monastery for more than 600 years.

The marvellous cultural achievements of the Cistercians are a resul of their special conception of monastic life. They lived, not from rev enues or land ownership, but by obtaining what they needed througl their own labour. As frequent choir practice compelled the monks to work fairly near to the monastery, they had to incorporate lay brother whose spiritual duties were not so great. The two groups lived com pletely separately in the monastery. From the 14th century the numbe of lay brothers constantly decreased. In their place, labour was hired, o the property was leased.

As time went by, the hard ascetic concept of the first flush of reforn was moderated, even for the Cistercians. Natural produce and mone poured into the monastery from more than two hundred towns and estates. While the growing wealth of the community made itself felt in spiritual life as much as did religious and social upheavals, monasti discipline never deteriorated. During the **Peasants' War**, the Abbe had already been forced to agree to dissolution for the general good in 1525, the peasants emptied the famous 'great barrel' containing ove 71,000 litres. War levies and military campaigns troubled the mona stery again and again, above all during the **Thirty Years' War**, In 1631 King *Gustav Adolf* of Sweden gave the monastery, which had beer deserted by the monks, to his Chancellor, *Axel Oxenstierna*; most of the library was lost, as were furnishings, works of art and stores. Not only Eberbach was affected, however; the many outer-lying estates were also destroyed. A long time was needed for the monastery to recove from its economic ruin. It only flourished again in the last century of its existence, which is evident in architectural renovations, new buildings

Stained-glass window (grisaille) with abstract plaited ornamentation from the monastery church, around 1180, Abbey museum ►

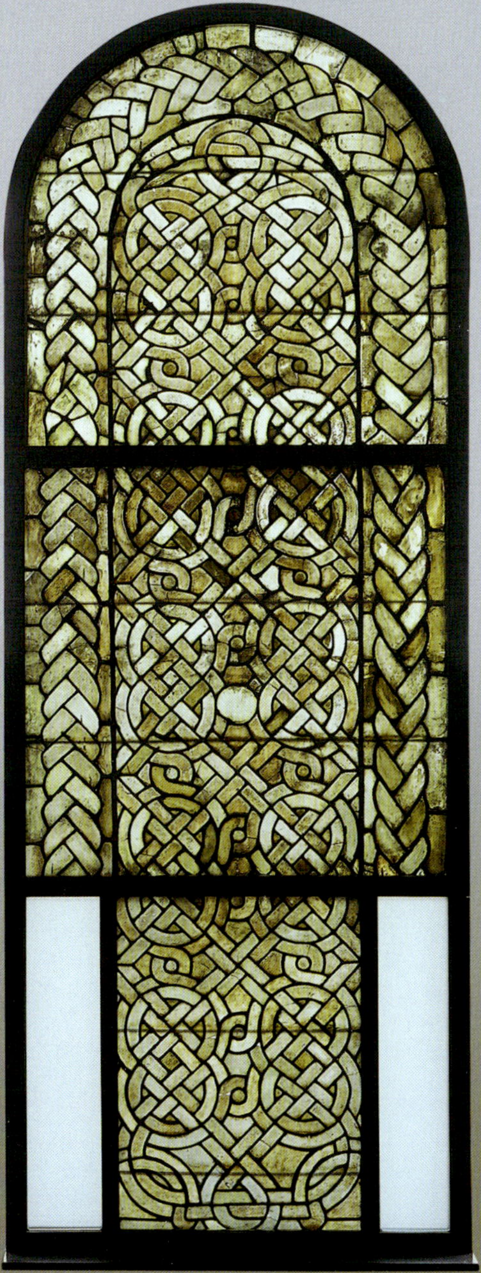

and the embellishment of the church in baroque style. But even before 1800, the decline had begun, because of the ever-decreasing economic resources caused by enormous taxes during the French Revolution. In the year 1802 the princely House of *Nassau-Usingen* received the Abbey in the course of **secularisation** as compensation for territorial losses to France on the left bank of the Rhine. On 18th September 1803, its **abolition** was decreed, and the monks left their spiritual home with a state pension. But, of course, in a changed world, even the Cistercians' cultural and spiritual light had grown dim; the existence of communities of monks as rich landlords had had its day.

Although Eberbach was not demolished after secularisation, as were many other great monastery complexes, the following century was a time of disfiguring changes and partial destruction. Only the vineyard and cellarage tradition, stretching back to the 12th century, was continued during the administration of Nassau. They and their successors – in 1866 the land fell to Prussia, and since 1945 it has belonged to the Land of Hessen – used the buildings on it. A prison occupied most of the grounds from 1813 to 1912, and at times also a psychatric hospital; from 1912 to 1918 a military convalescence home was established there. The repairs, initiated in 1926, aimed to reconstruct carefully the medieval condition and to remove structural defects. Since 1986, the State Building Office of Hesse in Wiesbaden (from 2004 onwards: Hessian Building Management), in close cooperation with the Hesse Office for the Preservation of Monuments and the current owner (until 1997: the state of Hesse; since 1998: Eberbach Monastery Foundation) has been carrying out a **general restoration** in several stages.

Cloister, west wing with library, from chapter-house ▶

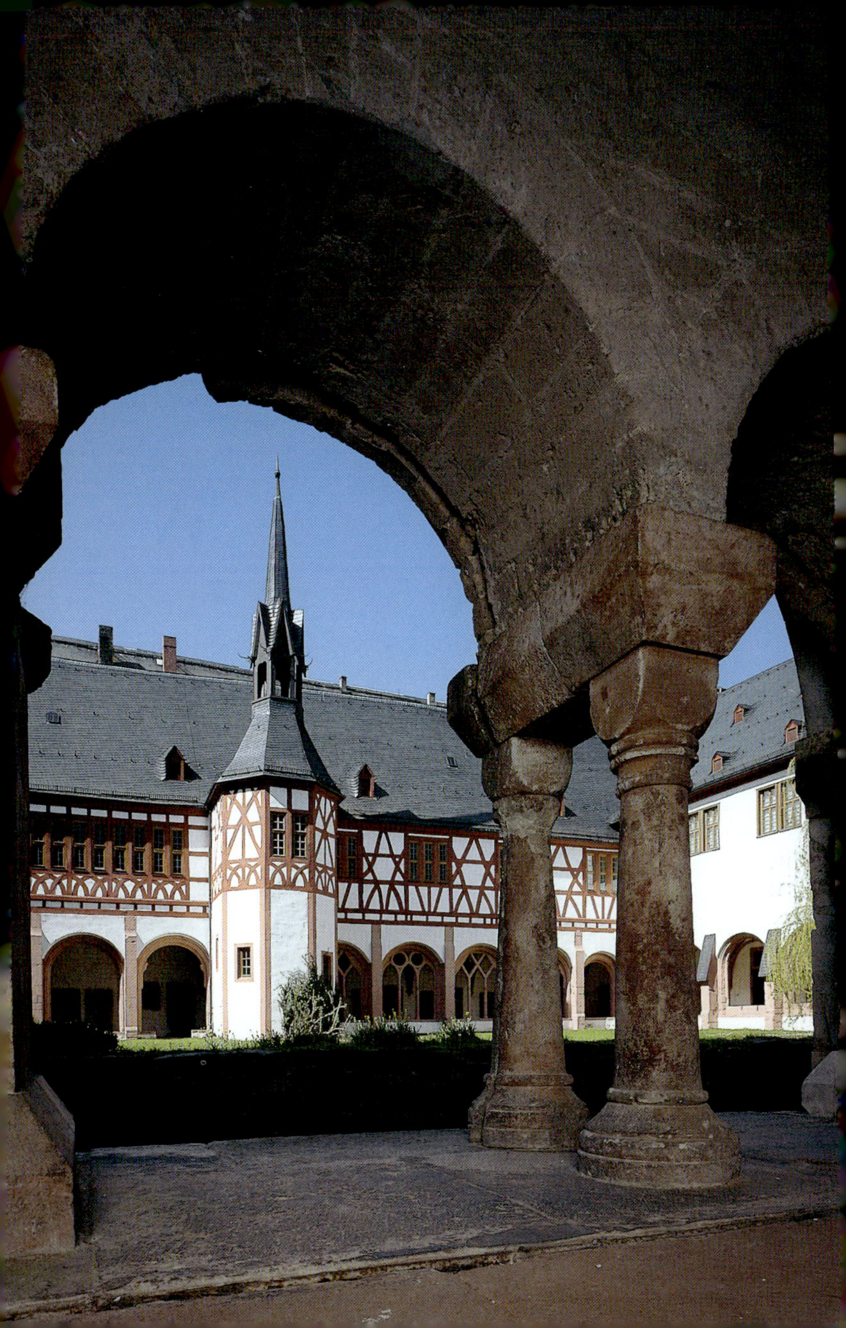

The Abbey complex

The red numbers in the text refer to the plan on page 23

Overview

The old monasteries in the Benedictine tradition were not only places of devotion, education, and of care for the poor and sick. In their seclusion they formed economically extensive independent communities. Like a small town, they surrounded themselves with gates and walls.

The **outer wall** of Eberbach is about 1100 metres long and 5 metres high. It has been preserved in its entirety and dates back to the 12th–13th century. Its daunting defensive appearance is interrupted by the tripartite **portal**, built in 1774 by the stonemason *Anton Süß* and the sculptor *Nikolaus Binterim* from Mainz, which, in its late baroque splendour, invites one into the monastery precincts. As patron saint of the Cistercian Order, **Maria Immaculata** stands raised above **John the Baptist**, the second patron saint of the Abbey, and the Order's own saint, **Bernard of Clairvaux**, the founder of Eberbach (copies; original in the Abbey museum). The Romanesque **porter's lodge** was rebuilt in 1740–41. On the outside, the Romanesque entrances have been preserved.

The **church** [**1**], the central point of the Abbey, towers above the monastery buildings with the baroque ridge turret over its crossing. Behind it is the **cloister quadrangle** [**2–9**], surrounding the cloister garden. This area was the exclusive reserve of the monks. To the west stretches the **lay brothers' building** [**12–14**], separated from the rest by the **Klostergasse** [**11**]. To the east of the Kisselbach stream lies the **hospital** [**22**], the building for the sick, at a distance from the rest. Later, under different circumstances the **new infirmary** [**21**] was built, providing a link with the cloister. The main buildings were thus grouped according to their order of importance to monastery life. Later, changed demands on space partly eliminated the clear structural divisions of the 12th–13th century, but apart from Eberbach, only Maulbronn can give us such a comprehensive idea of a large medieval Cistercian monastery complex in Germany.

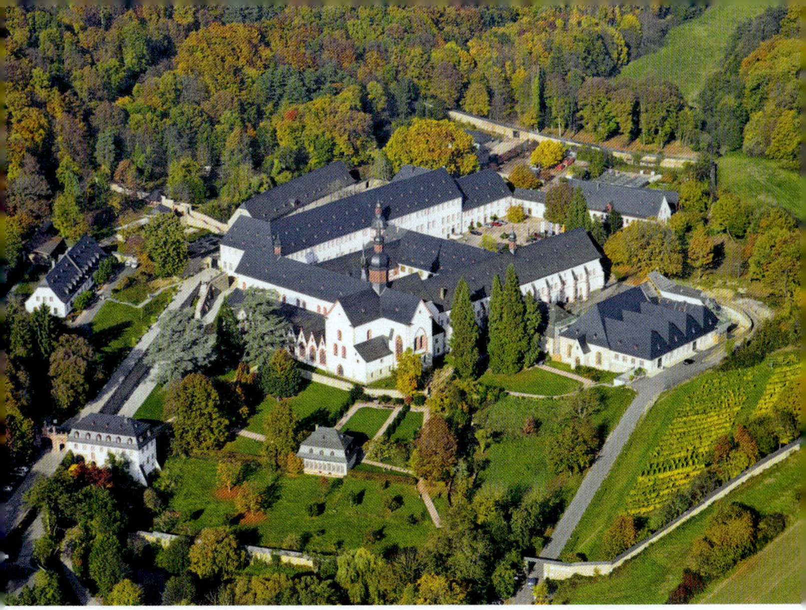

▲ *Aerial photograph of the monastery from the southeast. The cloister buildings are north of the monastery church, deviating from the Benedictine/Cistercian scheme.*

The monastery church

The **church** [**1**] which is desacralized today, was built during two periods: from around 1145 to 1160, and from about 1170 until its consecration in 1186. The first plans, modelled on the Burgundian parent monastery in Clairvaux, envisioned a building with squared-stone masonry, with a choir that stood lower than the nave and tunnel vaulting. Only the lower sections of the choir and the transept and the foundations of the church had been completed, however, before the building activity was interrupted after 1160, when the aftermath of the schism between Pope Alexander III and the Hohenstaufen Antipope reached the Middle Rhine region. The monastery was shaken by internal political disputes and confusion which resulted in the abbot's fleeing to Rome. Construction did not recommence until around 1170, by which time a new architectural plan had been adopted. The new rough-stone building had undecorated plastered walls of the same height, while the inner structure was different. This shows a stronger influence of Rhineland building traditions, while the austere Cistercian character was by no means abandoned. The monumental Romanesque forms are softened on the south by a row of 14th century chapels.

The interior of the **basilica** with its three aisles and its length of 79 metres is one of the least impaired examples of Romanesque architecture in Germany (fig. back cover). The very lack of all ornament clearly shows the architectural concepts of the Romanesque style. Hard, clear shapes are used everywhere: sharp-cornered, heavy pillars; simple Roman arches; smooth wall-surfaces; solid pilaster strips. The transept, with the strikingly low chapel entrances, gives a hint of the first plan of 1145, according to which the eastern parts should have been lower.

Of the works of art, only the **tombs** remain, some of which are among the most important works of their time. This is especially true of the tombstone at the eastern end of the southern chapel aisle, which memorialises the Cantor of the Mainz Cathedral, *Eberhard von Stein* († 1331), who is depicted bearing a mitre. Other exemplary works include the altar tomb lid of Count *Eberhard von Katzenelnbogen* († 1311) in the north transept, and the wall-tomb in the northern chancel wall, which has been preserved, although not in its original condition. The base and architectural framework belong to the canopied tomb of the Archbishop of Mainz, *Gerlach of Nassau* († 1371), whose tombstone now stands in the right-hand recess. This originally formed the horizontal end of the sarcophagus-like base. The almost incorporeal, narrow, extended figure, lying in a slightly curved position, is a splendid example of the idealised image of man of the 14th century. In lively contrast to this, there is, to the left, the tombstone from the tomb of the Archbishop of Mainz, *Adolph II von Nassau* († 1475), which was originally located in the choir area. Here the stretched-out corpse is realistically portrayed in the throes of death. Two tombs in the first south chapel from the west were probably created by *Hans Backoffen*, the most important sculptor in the Middle Rhine region during the transitional period from Gothic to Renaissance, and his workshop: that of *Wigand von Heinsberg* († 1511) and that of *Adam von Allendorf* († 1518) and his wife *Maria*

Tomb-chest for Archbishop Gerlach von Nassau (†1371) with the sepulchral slab of Archbishop Adolf II von Nassau (†1475), which was added to the left side in 1707 ▶

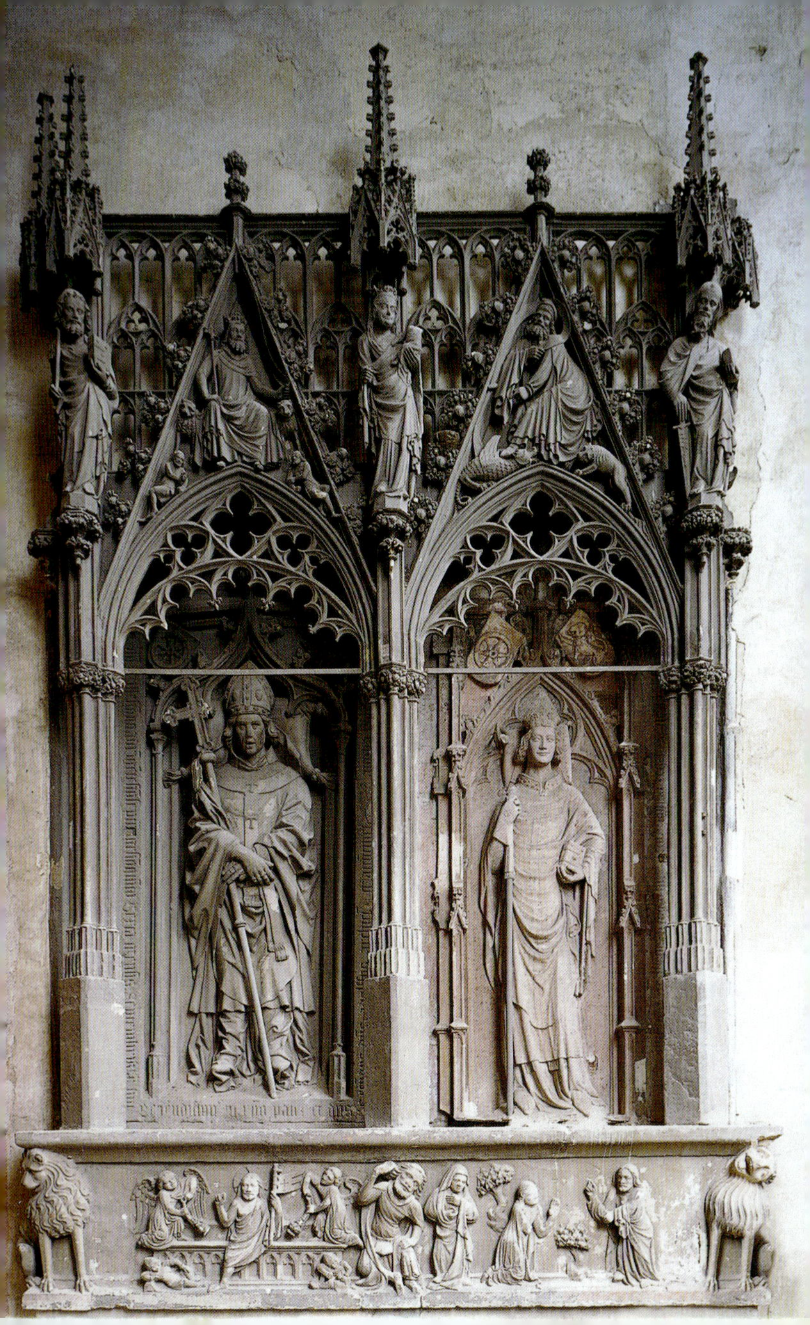

Specht von Bubenheim. Both works are interesting because of their partly Gothic, partly Renaissance borders and ornamentation. The sepulchral slabs of thirty abbots in the north aisle, arranged sequentially from the 14th to the 18th century, also make an impressive historical document. – A unique treasure from the church is the oldest preserved **stained-glass window** of the Cistercians in the German-speaking area (c. 1180, now in the Abbey museum), a so-called grisaille with plaited ornamentation (fig. p. 5).

The cloister buildings

The cloister buildings stretch out northwards from the church. This was a deviation from the Benedictine model that often occurred, due to problems with the building site. Here all the necessary rooms are grouped in a logical sequence and relation to the cloisters, around the cloister gardens.

The whole of the upper storey of the **east wing** is the **monks' dormitory**, which can be reached from the cloister and, more significantly, from the monks' chancel in the church, where a steep (night-)stairway led past the Abbot's cell (on the left) and the 'vault' (on the right). After the last evening Divine Office (compline), the monks laid themselves to sleep in their clothes on simple pallets until they were again called to the chancel shortly after midnight. The 72 metre-long pillared hall was built in c. 1250–70, and the south part by c. 1350. It is one of the most splendid early Gothic secular rooms in Europe. The removal of the original triple groups of pointed-arch windows is not so disturbing from the inside as from the outside, because the recesses, as well as the amount of light entering the hall, have remained almost unchanged. The original arrangement can still be seen opposite the central staircase. The rectangular windows were introduced around 1500 with the installation of cells, due to the diminished size of the flock that rested here. It was not until 1930–31 that the baroque cells in their completed form were removed, to enhance the uniform impression of the room.

On the ground floor in the northern part of the east wing there is another early Gothic room with two aisles, the **'Fraternei'**, or **Monks' Hall** [**5**], 47 metres long (open to the public during wine-tasting). The

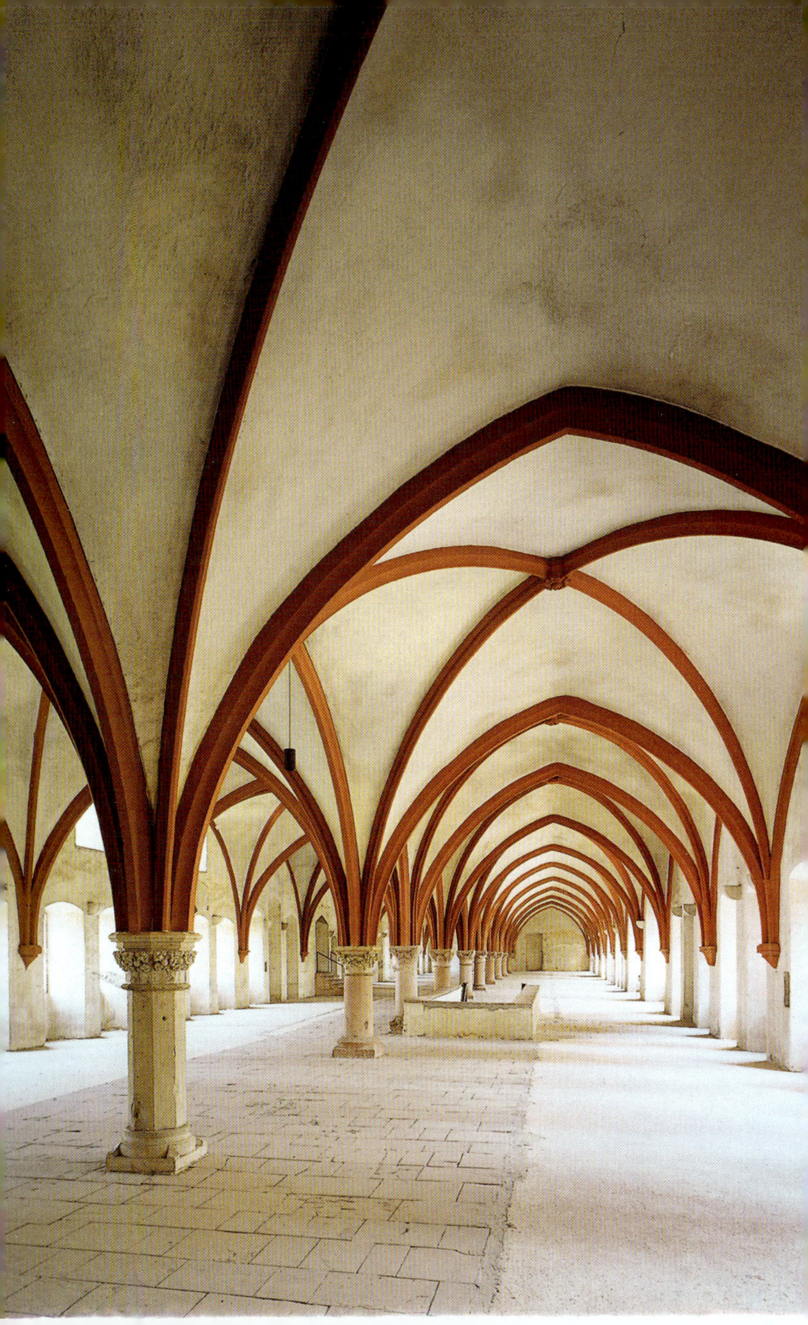

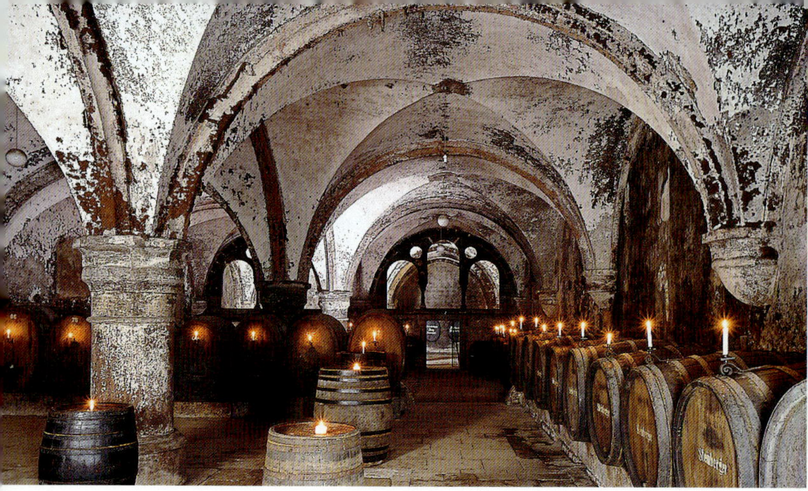

▲ *Fraternei (Monks' Hall) or Cabinetkeller (cabinett cellar)*

tracery windows, facing east, date it at 1240–50. During the course of the 13th century the monks' work took them less and less to field and vineyard, and large rooms suitable for domestic activities became necessary. Eberbach's 'Fraternei' is one of the few and oldest rooms of this type to have retained its impressive architectural form. The bricked-up windows give the room a solemn and oppressive air. It has been used as a wine-cellar since the end of the 15th century, at the latest. 'Kabinett', later to become a term defining the quality of wine, was first mentioned here in 1730 in the name **'Cabinetkeller'**.

In the southern part of the east wing, next to the church, are the Romanesque vestry and the early abbey library, the so-called **Armarium** [**2**], followed by the centrally situated **chapter-house** [**4**]. The name derives from the chapters, i.e. the statutes of the Order, which were always read out here. The hall served as a place for the meetings and deliberations of the community, and the abbots were also elected and buried here. Along with the areas beneath the windows on both sides, the chapter-house preserves for us a remnant of the old Romanesque monastery, finished in 1186. The beautiful star vault resting on a octogonal central pillar dates from about 1350.

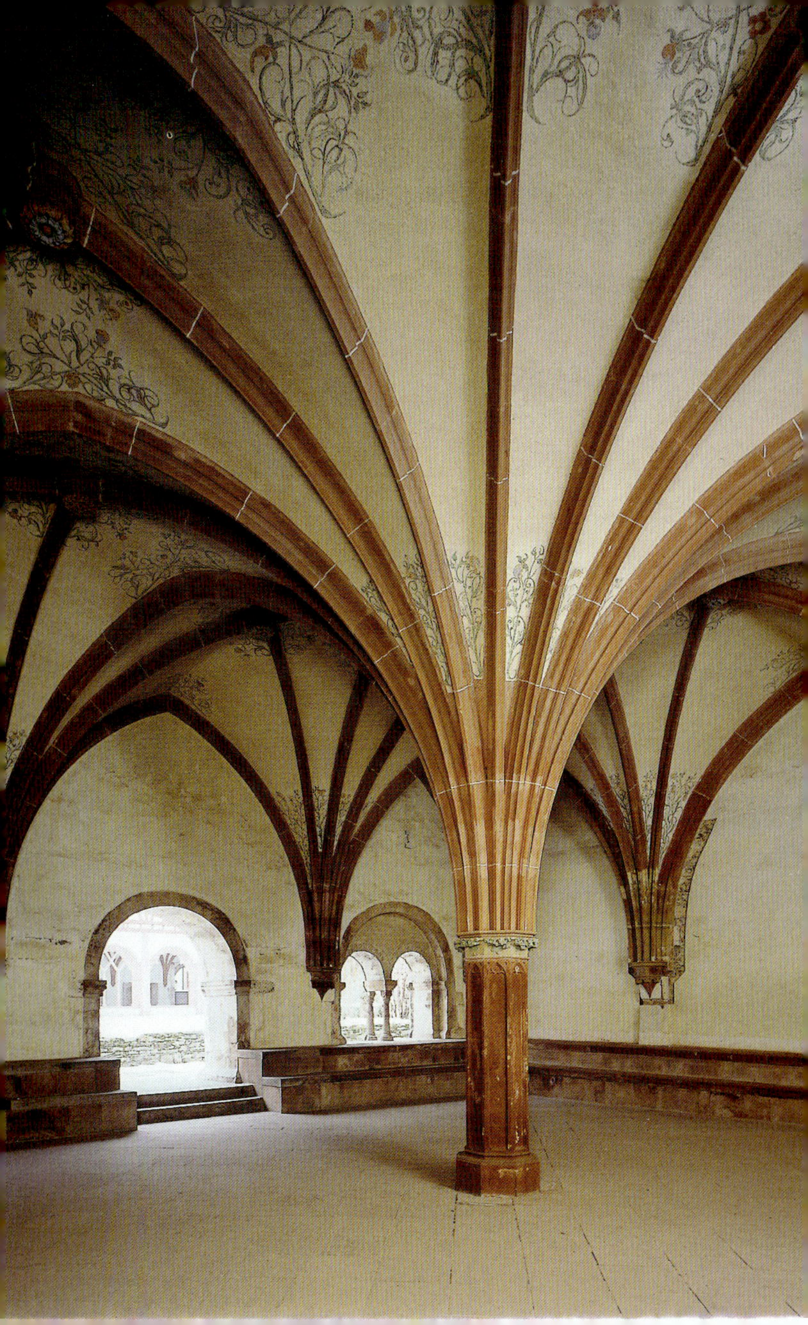

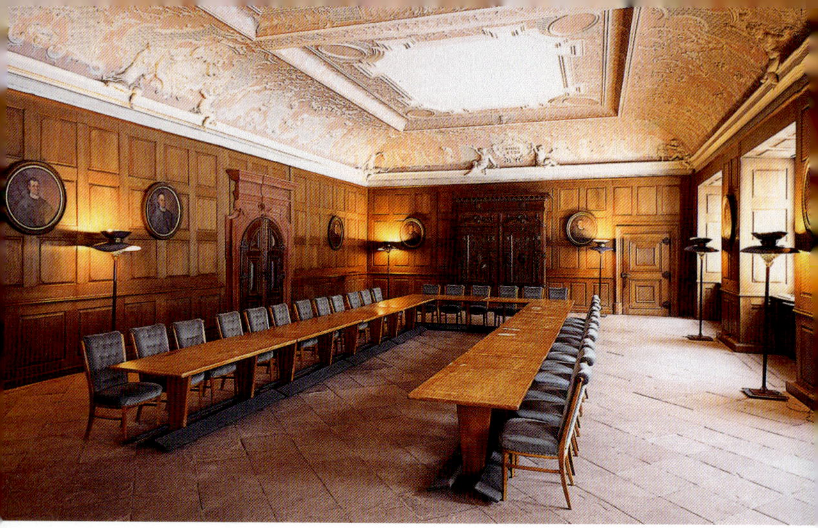

▲ *Monks' refectory*

Of the Romanesque **cloisters** [3] of the time before 1200, the western wall, facing the Klostergasse and the middle part of the present north wing of the cloisters, with its Roman arches opening onto the former **well-house** [8], are preserved. The only remaining traces of the well-house, which was characteristically Cistercian, are its foundations. All that remains of the 13th – 14th century Gothic cloisters are the west and north wings; the south and east wings were demolished in 1805. The rich tracery of the early Gothic period, similar to that on the 'Fraternei' windows, on the east side of the west wing of the lay brothers' cloister, has, however, been destroyed. The corbels of the vaulting in the east wing have richly-carved figures, e.g. the 'Eremite Reading', the adoration of Mary, patron saint of the order, by a Cistercian monk, and a 'girl angel' (some are copies, of which the originals are in the Abbey Museum). This was the last section of the cloisters to be built after the conversion of the chapter-house between 1350 and 1380.

The **northern wing** of the cloister buildings was completely rebuilt for the last time in 1720–1724 after plans by the Eberbach priest *Bernhard Kirn*, Because of this, and because of the extension and

Lay refectory with the historical wine-presses ▶

enlargement of the cloisters, it is only by close inspection that one can see that remains of the Romanesque monastery of the time before 1186 still exist, above all the imposing portal of the refectory. Even after the reconstructions in the baroque period, the monks used this as an entrance to their new dining-hall. The **monks' refectory** [7], by virtue of its magnificent stuccoed ceiling built by unknown Masters from Mainz in 1738, is the only representative baroque room in the monastery. The ornate late Renaissance cupboard with the monastery's canting arms dates from the first half of the 17th century. The **Romanesque refectory** [6], a double-aisled hall, used to extend far to the north. The **kitchen** [9] also dates back to the Romanesque period, as does the room above it, which probably served as a warming-parlor. Here, the monks could occasionally find refuge from the cold.

In c. 1480, a **library** in heavy, late-Gothic timber-framing was built above the west wing of the cloisters (fig. p. 7). It is connected to the cloisters through a spiral staircase. In the southern part, there was a 20 metres long book room with a gallery; in the centre was the enormous archives, visible from the Klostergasse, followed by several rooms for noble guests. The entire floor, and the corresponding floor in the north wing, have been the **Abbey museum** since 1995.

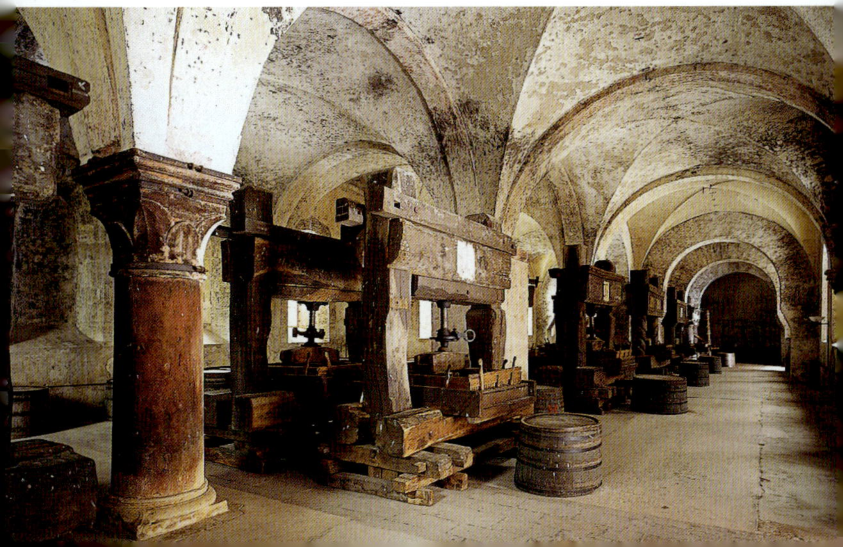

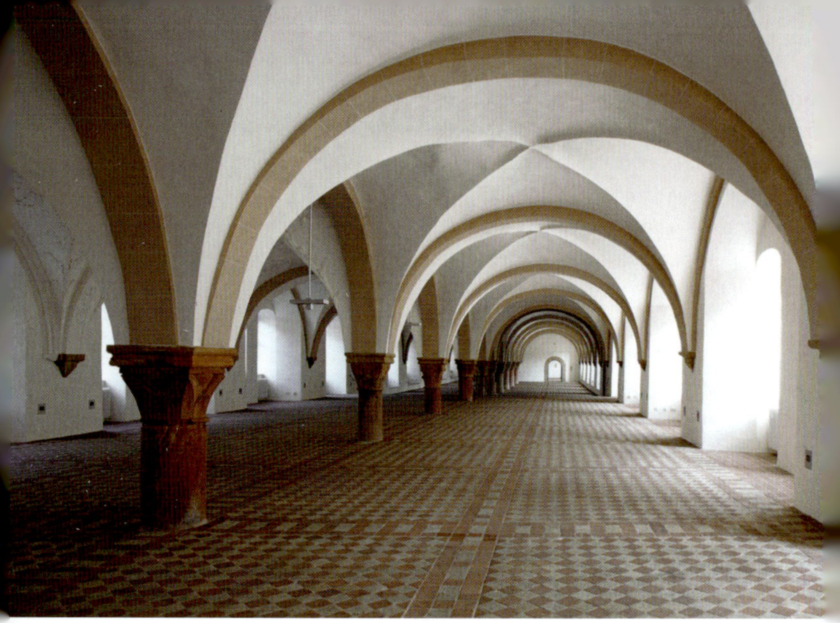

▲ *Lay dormitory*

To the west of the monks' cloister and separated from it by the **Klostergasse** [**11**] rises the **lay brothers' cloister** [**12–14**], begun before 1200 and completed at the beginning of the 13th century. This enormous building, which had two storeys until the 18th century, contained all the rooms necessary for the lay brothers, and also, in the northern part of the ground floor, the **monastery's cellar** [**14**]. A **barrel-vaulted corridor** [**13**] leads through the centre of the ground floor, and this was originally an important entrance to the inner sections of the monastery. There is no comparable existing lay building in the whole of Cistercian architecture.

The southern part contains the 45-metre **lay refectory** [**12**]. The vaulting in this dining-room, which was renewed in 1709, rests on mainly roughly-finished pillars, of which only one is completely free-standing. This measure became necessary for structural reasons, when a storey was added to the building in the early 18th century. The wine-presses installed there go back to Cistercian times; the oldest dates from 1668, the youngest from 1801. The upper storey contains only one pillared hall with two aisles, the **lay dormitory**, which, at 83 metres, is bigger than the monks' dormitory, and the biggest secular room of the Romanesque period in Europe. This is where the famous traditional wine auctions take place, in addition to a wealth of other cultural events. When the number of lay brothers decreased during the course of the Middle Ages, the building was used for other purposes. It is recorded that the refectory was used as a wine-cellar from 1501. From 1707–08, this apartment was converted into a prestigious **prelacy** [**20**]. The present outer appearance of the lay brothers' building dates from the first half of the 18th century, when a third storey was added, containing the more convenient administrative and working buildings (burse) of the monks. The lay brothers' dining-room and dormitory were again restored to an approximation of their Romanesque condition as part of the restoration work that has continued since 1926.

To the east, outside the cloister, lies the **new infirmary** [**21**], a plain baroque building of 1752–53. This is now the main entrance for visitors. The building joins onto the **hospital** [**22**], which has served as a wine-cellar since at least the early 17th century. The hospital, built 1215–20, in the area where, around 1116, the Augustinian canons had established their small religious settlement, completed the Cistercians' plan for a great Romanesque monastery. Although the façade is still Romanesque, originally with two rows of Romanesque windows, one set above the other, along the sides, the interior is a high, pillared hall with three aisles, the internal diameter of which testifies its links with the early Gothic. Apart from the hospital of the former Cistercian monastery Ourscamp (Dép. Oise), which is used as a church, the hospital at Eberbach provides the only example in Europe, of a magnificent medieval monastic hospital from the 'golden age' of the Cistercian Order, because it has never been altered by reconstruction or extensions. To the north of the hospital is a wide, two-storied 14th century building with a façade resembling a late Gothic noble **residence** [**24**]. Within the hospital complex it was probably used for prebendaries, who could acquire the right to live here in old age. Of particular inte-

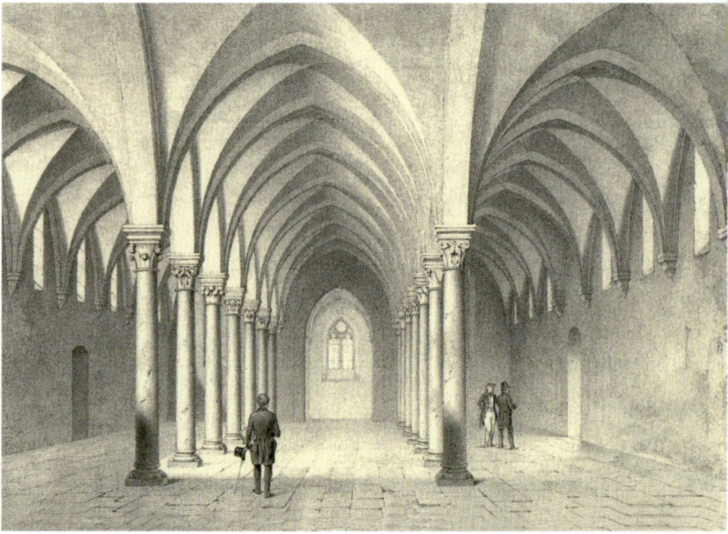

▲ *Hospital, idealised lithograph from around 1850*

rest is the small hall on the ground floor. Its ceiling is supported by a strong wooden pillar.

The main buildings of the Abbey were surrounded by **outbuildings**, as was required for the independence of the monastery, which was like a self-contained town. Those which remain date back only to the late 17th century. Following a thorough renovation, they are now used in part by the monastery hotel and hotel restaurant.

Eberbach Monastery today: living cultural heritage in the spirit of many traditions

Today, Eberbach Monastery is a **charitable foundation** under public law whose mission is to preserve the abbey buildings for posterity and to keep them open for the public and for cultural purposes. Although the last monks had to leave Eberbach approximately 200 years ago, this mission takes up a number of monastic traditions that were once fostered here. A Cistercian's Day takes place here every year and provides an impressive reflection of Eberbach's spiritual and cultural sources.

The Eberbach Monastery Foundation as the owner of the complex therefore endeavours to maintain all the historically important buildings in good condition in the course of a comprehensive **general restoration** and, where necessary, to restore them as far as possible to their original appearance as documented. This project is financed by the government of Hesse; all other costs of maintaining the buildings and running the buildings are borne by the Foundation. The entrance fees and the income from leasing rooms and the restaurant or selling books and information material are used for this purpose.

Eberbach Monastery is used for **cultural activities** of the most varied kind, at present musical and winegrowing functions in particular. In the basilica and in the lay dormitory, for example, many concerts are held every year. Particularly famous are the functions of the *Rheingau Music Festival*, usually including the opening and closing concerts, and the *Eberbach Monastery Sunday concerts*.

In addition, the furnishings of some central rooms (lay refectory, cabinet cellar and hospital cellar), and the wine auctions held every spring and autumn, recall the Cistercians' almost 700-year-old **winegrowing tradition**. This tradition is also preserved by the Hessen Government Winegrowing Estates, which managed the monastery buildings until 1997. Since 2008, they have maintained a well-stocked ***vinothek*** in the former **wine press room** [**26**] adjacent to the Hospital and have relocated their winery from Eltville to the monks' main vineyard, the Steinberg, before the gates of the abbey.

Several rooms of varying size are available as a **forum for talks, seminars and deliberations.** This practice is intended to take up the tradition of intellectual exchange, which was always an important element in the network of monasteries of the Cistercian order.

If you are planning to take a guided tour of Eberbach Monastery, to take part in a monastery tour with accompanying wine tasting or to lease specific rooms for a private function – including the possibility to marry in the cloister's own romantic registry office –, please contact

Stiftung Kloster Eberbach
D-65346 Eltville · Tel. +49 (0) 67 23/91 78-100 · Fax -101
Internet: www.klostereberbach.de
E-mail: info@klostereberbach.de

Daily opening times for tours:
Beginning of April until the end of October: 10 a.m. – 6 p.m.
Beginning of November until the end of March: 11 a.m. – 5 p.m.
The monastery may be visited without a guide. There are regular guided tours from April until October on Fridays at 3 p.m. and at weekends at 11 a.m., 1 p.m. and 3 p.m.; from November until March on Saturdays and Sundays at 2 p.m. Guided tours for groups only by arrangement.
Vinothek with shop: Daily 10 a.m. – 6 p.m.

Photographs: Florian Monheim, Krefeld. – p. 9: Thomas Ott, www.o2t.de. – p. 20: Archive, Deutscher Kunstverlag.
Printed by F&W Mediencenter, Kienberg
Translated by Christine Perks, revised by Kerstin Hall and Allegra Silbiger
Cover photograph: *Monastery church (basilica) from the southeast*
Back cover: *Monastery church, nave, looking west*

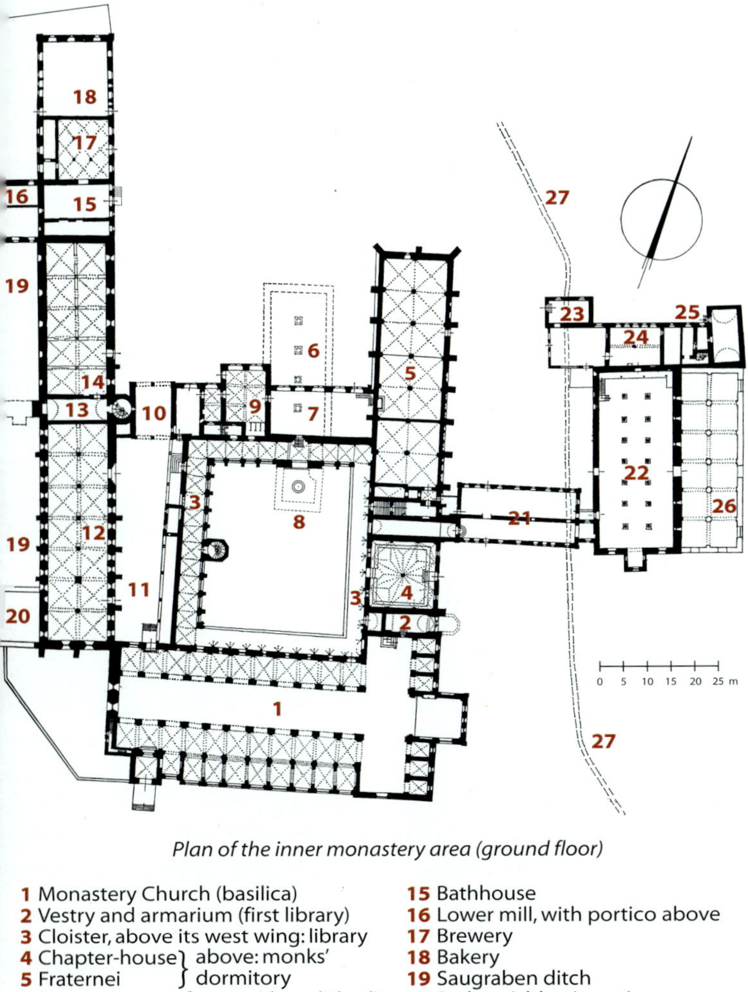

Plan of the inner monastery area (ground floor)

1 Monastery Church (basilica)
2 Vestry and armarium (first library)
3 Cloister, above its west wing: library
4 Chapter-house } above: monks' dormitory
5 Fraternei
6 Romanesque refectory (demolished)
7 Baroque Monks' refectory
8 Well-house (demolished)
9 Kitchen (now vestibule) with side rooms, above, the "warming parlor"
10 Portico
11 Klostergasse
12 Lay refectory } above: lay dormitory
13 Romanesque monastery entrance
14 Cellar
15 Bathhouse
16 Lower mill, with portico above
17 Brewery
18 Bakery
19 Saugraben ditch
20 Prelacy (abbot's seat)
21 New infirmary and priory (tour entrance)
22 Hospital (guest house)
23 Slaughterhouse
24 Prebendaries' house
25 Ice cellar
26 Wine vault, above the wine press room (now *vinothek*), 19th – 20th c.
27 Kisselbach stream

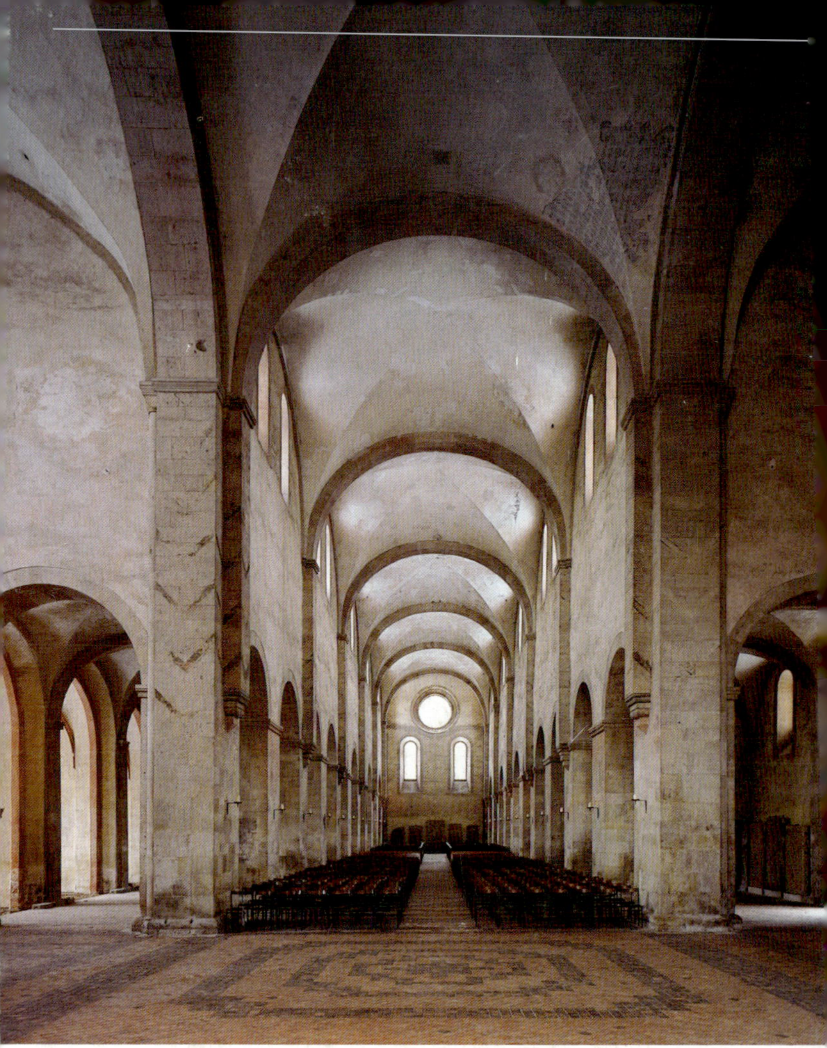

DKV ART GUIDE No. 267
Tenth rev. Edition 2013 · ISBN 978-3-422-02165-5

Nymphenburger Straße 90e · D-80636 München
www.deutscherkunstverlag.de

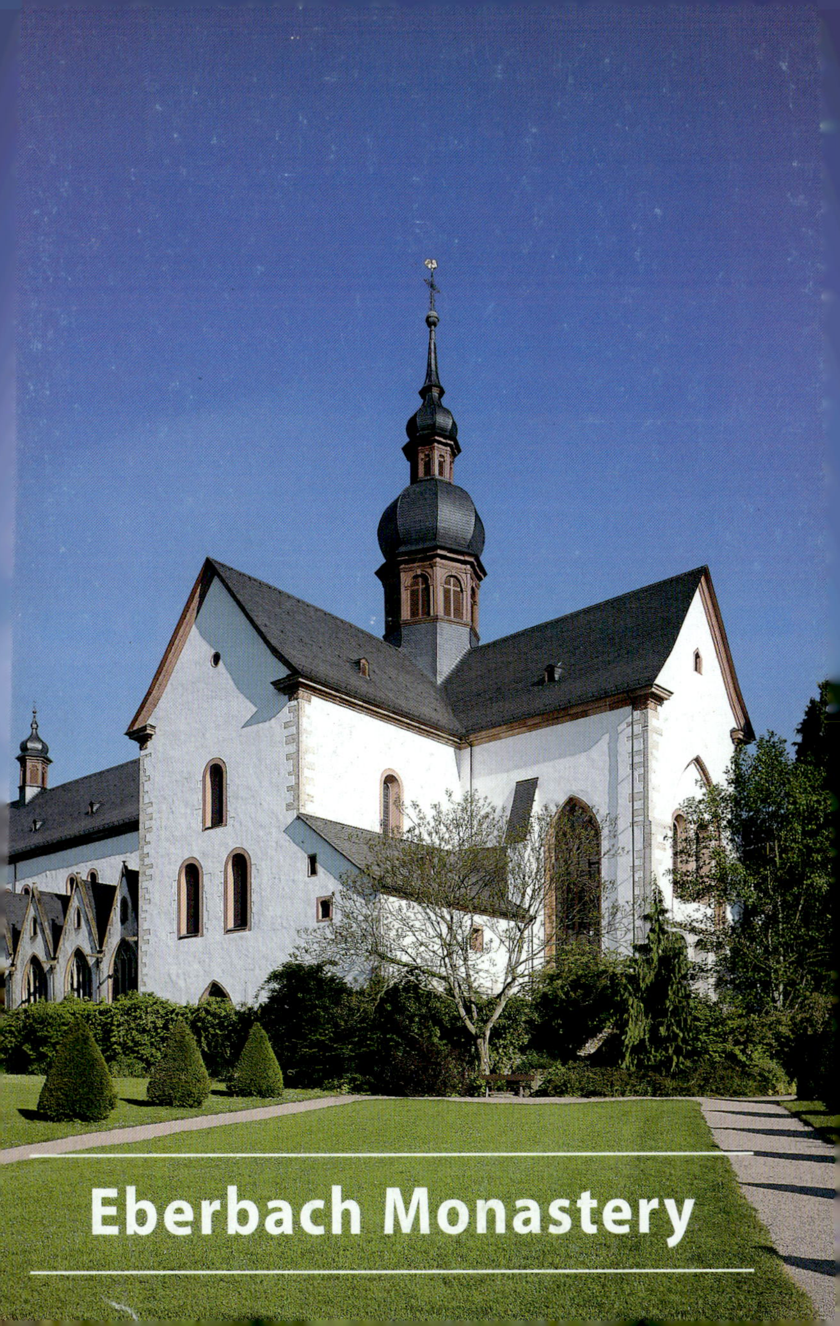

Eberbach Monastery

Eberbach Monastery

by Wolfgang Einsingbach (†),
revised and updated
by Wolfgang Riedel

To the north of the Rheingau, where the Taunus Mountains shelter the vineyards, a walled monastery lies at the lower end of the Kisselbach valley. Far below the village settlements, in dark contrast, once stronger than now, to the charming landscape along the river, the group of monastery buildings preserves something of the seclusion which was the way of life for the community of monks who lived there for 700 years.

The Cistercian Order and the History of the Monastery

When the **Cistercians** established their colony in Eberbach in 1136, the Order was expanding rapidly, under the leadership of the charismatic abbot *Bernard of Clairvaux* (c. 1090–1153). He sent monks from his Burgundian monastery to settle in Eberbach. Through his faith, organisational talent and rousing sermons, the whole western world responded to the piety of the Benedictine monastic reform movement, which began only in 1098. When Bernard died in 1153, he left behind him hundreds of settlements. The old 6th-century Benedictine monastic rules were rigorously followed everywhere. Only a few hours sleep interrupted the cycle of choir practice and hard work. Silent, apart from the most necessary communications, the monks lived on meagre diets, in draughty, unheated rooms.

The monks who were summoned by Archbishop *Adalbert* of Mainz in 1136 found a settlement which had been in existence since 1116. **Augustinian canons** and, from 1131, **Benedictines** had lived there before them, but only under the **Cistercians** did the monastery flourish. They found here the ideal conditions for their Spartan life.

View into the cloister, looking towards the Rhine Valley ▶

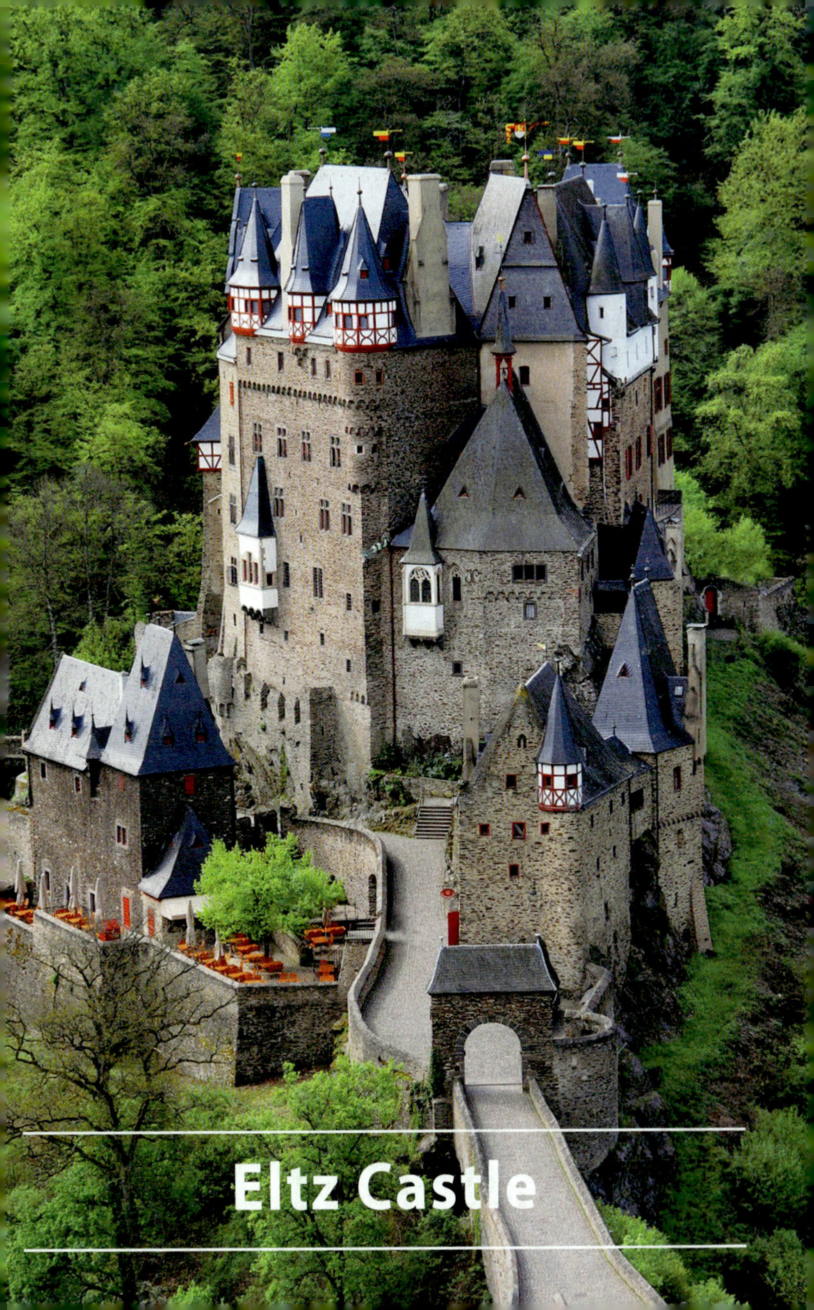

Eltz Castle

Eltz Castle

by Dieter Ritzenhofen

»Eltz Castle is ›the castle par excellence‹. Its solitude and the beauty of its situation stimulate the imagination« (Georg Dehio)

Mediaeval castles which we now admire for their romantic atmosphere began to develop in the 9th and 10th century. What had previously been manor houses with protective earth walls and palisades became well-fortified castles surrounded by strong defensive walls. Castle building had its heyday from the late 11th to 13th century, the period of the Hohenstaufen. Apart from the many castles, numerous townships were founded. The name of **Eltz** was first mentioned during this period. The Emperor's officer, *Rudolph von Eltz*, is mentioned as witness in a deed of gift of Emperor Frederick I Barbarossa in 1157. Parts of the castle in which Rudolph von Eltz lived were the Late Romanesque tower with living quarters, keep **Platt Eltz** [7], and the remains of the Romanesque house in the lower floor of the Kempenich House seen clearly from the Romanesque double arch uncovered during restoration work in 1978. A cistern was built to supply the castle with water. It is now below the mighty stair tower of the Kempenich House.

The highly strategic position of the Lower Elz (or Eltz), a tributary of the Moselle, was undoubtedly decisive when building this first castle. It was built on a route which linked the Moselle, always one of the most important trade routes, with the Eifel and the fertile »Maifeld«.

The 70 m high, elliptical head of rock forms the foundation of the entire castle. The rock is surrounded on three sides by the Eltz. The castle's ground plan, therefore, is oval in keeping with the natural features.

The first division of the family into three lines, those of the brothers *Elias, Wilhelm* and *Theoderich*, took place before the year 1268. The castle and its lands were also divided. According to their coats-of-arms, these three main lines of the house of Eltz were called **»Eltz vom goldenen Löwen«**, **»Eltz vom silbernen Löwen«** and **»Eltz von den Büffelhörnern«**. The separate lines then lived together as joint heirs in

The figures in brackets refer to the ground plan on page 23